THE NATURE OF GRIEF

Photographs and Words
for Reflection and Healing

By Rebecca S. Hauder, R.N., M.Ed.

Published by Resources for Grief™
Boise, ID 83702
www.resourcesforgrief.com

THE NATURE OF GRIEF

Photos and Text: Rebecca S. Hauder, R.N., M.Ed

For information, contact Resources for Grief, 1674 Hill Rd., Suite 14, Boise, ID 83702; 208-336-0200, www.resourcesforgrief.com
email: info@resourcesforgrief.com.

ISBN-1-4392-6438-4
Printed in the United States of America

Acknowledgements

Thanks to Larry, my husband of 39 years, for supporting my writing endeavors through his business savvy and eye for words. Also, thanks to my family and friends who continue to honor and encourage my creativity.

Finally, I am indebted to the many grieving persons who have shared their stories and tears. They have taught me most of what I know about the nature of loss and grief.

Contents

The Healing Power of Nature

During times of confusion and uncertainty, I walk to the arid hills surrounding Boise or drive north to the shores of Idaho's Payette Lake. Here I am reminded of the cycles and beauty of nature, its mystery and its connection to the Divine. In nature I find renewal, a primal kind of comfort, and a sense of stability. The Spirit's "still small voice" has more volume here, and I regain perspective.

Experience for yourself the healing potential in nature as you reflect on the following photographs and accompanying text. Some of the 12 suggestions may be relevant to what you are feeling now; other parts you may want to save for later. The ideas are gleaned from 25 years of counseling the bereaved and from professional peers with expertise in grief and loss.

May these pages serve as a guide for your own unique journey of grief, and provide inspiration to seek out the nature "sanctuaries" near you!

—Rebecca S. Hauder

"There is no grief that time does not lessen and soften."
—Cicero

12 Suggestions for Healing Your Grief

"Speak to the earth
and it shall teach thee."
—Job 12:8 (O.T.)

"Love knows not its depth until the hour of separation."
—Kahlil Gibran

1. Provide Gentle Self-Care

Following the death of a loved one, there is often a flurry of activity, with friends and family coming together, food delivered, and services to arrange. Later, business matters and thank-you notes beg for attention. You may go through the motions detached, numb, and with a sense of disbelief. This allows you to absorb the depth and impact of your loss in small doses.

All the commotion and upheaval produces exhaustion, made worse if you had been the caregiver during a long illness. Difficulty sleeping and eating are the norm, as is trouble focusing. Grief does involve many dimensions of life!

When grief is fresh, don't try to go it alone. Ask others for assistance with tasks or to simply be present. If you're not hungry at mealtime, eat one item of food every few hours, and drink plenty of fluids. Before bed, take a soothing bath or sip a cup of warm milk. Know that the grief journey won't always be this difficult. You will eventually adjust and heal, but it will be in your own unique way and time.

"Blessed are those who mourn, for they will be comforted."
—Jesus of Nazareth

2. Identify Common Grief Responses

Many people find it easier to accept the grief experience when they realize their reactions are normal and natural. Perhaps you will identify with some of these common responses:

- Shock and Disbelief: At first, the death feels like a bad dream.
- Numb: Feelings for anything or anybody are missing.
- Anxiety and Fear: There's worry for the future and what might happen.
- Anger: It may be towards yourself, the one who died, caregivers, or God.
- Relief: If there's been a long illness, the burden is lifted; you feel lighter.
- Guilt and Regret: "What if" and "if only" keep circling in your mind.
- Sad and Lonely: Day-to-day life has a big empty hole in it.
- Jealous: Others still have their loved ones; this doesn't seem fair.
- Restless: Starting anything new seems futile; it's just not worth it.
- Confused: Concentrating is difficult and forgetting things is easy.
- Overwhelmed: There is so much to do, yet so little energy and focus.

"Sorrow like a river must be given vent lest it erode its bank."
—Chinese Proverb

3. Find an Outlet for the Feelings

A range of intense emotions and reactions can be generated after a major loss. Anger, rage, guilt, fear, and anxiety are powerful feelings that can be especially difficult. A natural response is to try to keep a lid on these feelings, sometimes with the help of alcohol or other addictions, or by simply keeping busy. Sooner or later, however, suppressing emotions takes a physical and emotional toll. The Roman poet, Ovid, as far back as 1600, wrote, "Suppressed grief suffocates, and is forced to multiply its strength."

When confronted with the emotions surrounding grief, pay attention! The body often carries the first cues—a knot in the stomach or a tense jaw, for example. Also, name what you are feeling: "I feel guilty I wasn't there when he died." Finally, find safe and effective outlets for the feelings through such means as crying, walking, running, talking, painting, or writing. Feelings that are identified and expressed tend to lessen in intensity. Keep in mind, strong emotions may resurface from time to time. However, with proper attention, they're unlikely to persist.

"To fashion an inner story of our pain carries us to the heart of it,
which is where rebirth inevitably occurs." —Sue Monk Kidd

4. Keep a Journal

Consider keeping a personal journal during these difficult times. A journal provides a safe place to reflect on what has happened and helps you begin the healing process. Research shows that it also relieves stress and boosts the body's immune system. Some guidelines can help you get started:

- Choose any type of notebook and a favorite pen, or use a computer.
- Write for 10-20 minutes a day and whenever you feel the urge.
- Choose a place to write that is comfortable and private.
- Set the mood with background music and a candle, if that helps.
- Write without attention to grammar, spelling, or making sense.
- Make journal entries in list form, if you prefer—jotting down emotions, memories, plans, or ideas.
- Depict feelings with markers or crayons when words aren't adequate.
- Write a letter to your loved one describing the relationship you shared, including what you cherish and what you regret, or express whatever is on your heart in a letter to another person or to God.

"Love is a fruit in season at all times, and within reach
of every hand." —Mother Teresa

5. Care for Your Whole Being

Grief affects many aspects of your being, including the body, mind, and spirit. Because so many dimensions of life are impacted, you may lose self-confidence and believe you are somehow flawed. Giving yourself the love and respect you deserve can help to rebuild the sense of worth and dignity that may have been lost, however. Here are some ideas to get you started:

- Make a medical appointment if you're due for a physical exam.
- Arrange for a massage or some other form of relaxation.
- Break need-to-do tasks into small parts, and be sure to rest at intervals.
- Take note of self-critical thoughts, replacing them with positive ones.
- Put encouraging statements about yourself on the bathroom mirror.
- Realize the pain of grief can obscure your relationship with the Divine.
- Accept the humanness of sorrow; it does not imply spiritual weakness.
- Utilize inspirational readings and prayers that bring comfort.
- Seek direction and support from a counselor, pastor, or spiritual guide.
- Show close friends and family that you still love and care for them too!

"Walking with a friend in the dark is better than walking alone in the light." —Helen Keller

6. Seek Ongoing Support

At first, after a death, friends tend to rally around, offering an overwhelming show of support. However, as time goes on, the calls and visits tend to taper off, usually when they are needed most. Your friends are getting on with their lives, and they may assume you are too.

Grieving is a lengthy journey, and encouragement is needed from those who understand this reality. Being able to confide in others without feeling judged is also beneficial. Consider who provides you this kind of support. Is it a family member, friend, neighbor, coworker, or spiritual leader?

If your support seems adequate, thank those who are there for you! If your support is lacking, however, try developing new friendships, perhaps with persons who have had similar experiences. To meet others, consider joining an organization or club, volunteering for a local agency, attending religious services, or signing up for a grief support group. Reaching out takes a lot of courage, but the potential rewards are well worth the effort.

"Grief changes the rules, and sometimes rearranges the combinations." —Martha Whitmore Hickman

7. Make Needed Adjustments

There are many adjustments following a major loss. Routines, roles, and relationships are altered, as well as long-held beliefs. There might be one less table setting to put out at mealtime, new and challenging responsibilities, or a change in role from that of spouse to being a widow. The notion that your death would be first is no longer valid either.

Try making a list of the ways your life has been affected since the death. How have routines changed? Relationships and roles? Assumptions about life? These changes represent secondary losses, and you grieve those too.

Know that in time you will adjust, especially with an open and flexible attitude, and a willingness to risk doing things differently than in the past. Letting go of familiar ways of thinking or doing to embrace new perspectives and fresh possibilities takes courage. But without adapting and changing, growth stagnates, life shrinks, and you sacrifice what life could become.

"When we are no longer able to change a situation, we are challenged to change ourselves." —Viktor Frankl

8. Manage the Stress of Change

The death of a loved one can be the most stressful of life events, and there may be a variety of symptoms to prove it! Headaches, indigestion, irritability, insomnia, depressed mood, fatigue, anxiety, and muscle aches are some of the common stress signals. Over time, these can cause more serious health problems. To lower that risk, try this three-step approach:

1. Make a list of the things that trigger a stress response.

2. Do something about the situations you can change or eliminate. For instance, delay major decisions until there is more focus and clarity, and when possible, turn over dreaded or difficult tasks to someone else.

3. Cultivate an inner calm when you cannot change a situation: Breathe deeply for 1-2 minutes, counting to 4 as you inhale and as you exhale; engage in an enjoyable or life-giving activity, slow down, relax your standards, choose battles carefully, and list the things for which you are grateful.

"You are not lost. You continue in every hearty laugh, in every nice surprise, and in every reassuring moment of my life." —Molly Fuima

9. Embrace the Memories

Death ends a life, but it doesn't end a relationship. The person you loved is present in many moments of daily life, and you will continue to be reminded of him or her throughout each day. While the intensity of grief may ebb and flow, a loved one's impact won't ever be forgotten, particularly if the memories are nurtured and cultivated.

To nurture memories, talk or write about favorite times, retain special keepsakes, display photos, create a memory book, contribute to a worthy cause, visit the places where you used to go, have your loved one's jewelry made into an item you will wear, or place a park bench in their name. And consider inviting children and others who grieve to share in these activities.

When many of the memories are unpleasant, finding ways to honor a loved one is difficult. If that is your situation, explore and air out the hurts and resentments. Then, as a gift to yourself, choose to let them go, so that in time you can move forward without carrying burdens from the past.

"You are never too old to set another goal or to dream
a new dream." —C.S. Lewis

10. Search for Meaning

Life often seems less certain after the death of someone near. A world that seemed relatively secure may now appear shaken and in disarray. As a result, you may wonder what significance and purpose life now holds.

You may be asking questions like these: "Who am I apart from my loved one?" "What do I have to look forward to?" "Where will I find meaning?" "How will I ever be able to love again?" Your life has changed and it's quite legitimate to have doubts and uncertainties.

Allow the questions—you may even want to jot them down—but don't pressure yourself to find the answers right now. Direction for the next chapter will emerge slowly and over time. For now, let yourself live with a heart and mind that is open to many possibilities, but also present in the activities of today—whether reading this book, getting dressed, doing the dishes, talking to a friend, or walking the dog.

"Grief comes in unexpected surges...crashing like a wave, sweeping me in its crest..." —Toby Talbot

11. Prepare for Special Occasions

On anniversaries, holidays, changes of season, and other special occasions, grief can crash in on you like an immense ocean wave! Plan ahead for those times and you are less likely to be caught off-guard.

1. Create a plan as you anticipate an event. Decide how and with whom you want to commemorate or celebrate that day. Know it's okay to do something totally different than you've done in years past, or decide not to celebrate at all if it will be too painful this year.

2. Use simple rituals to remember your loved one. Burn a candle, go to the cemetery, place a rose on the table, reminisce, make your loved one's favorite dessert, or do something he or she would have enjoyed.

3. Accept whatever mood you're in. Laugh and have fun, if you feel like it. On the other hand, you don't have to feel or act happy, even if it's a holiday. You have the right to both laughter and tears without feeling guilty.

"However long the night, the dawn will break."
—African Proverb

12. Believe Life is Worth Living

The journey of grief doesn't have a calendar or a specific destination. But the time will come when you will able to embrace past memories, even as you live fully in the present and look forward to a life of renewed meaning and purpose.

To progress towards healing, continue to do the following: Listen to your feelings, accept what cannot be changed, do something each day that nourishes your spirit, give time to others, enjoy the confidence you're gaining, keep trusting in a higher power, and don't hesitate to seek professional counseling if you think it could be beneficial.

Finally, accept this sacred blessing, adapted from the Bible's Old Testament:

> *May the Spirit bless and take care of you.*
> *May the Spirit show kindness and have mercy on you.*
> *May the Spirit watch over you and give you peace.*

Your Personal Reflections
Record quotes, thoughts, ideas, feelings, poems, prayers, or gratitudes.

Your Personal Reflections

"There is no way to grieve; there is just your way." —Unknown

When to Seek Professional Help

Contact your healthcare provider if you are:
1. Having persistent thoughts of hurting yourself or someone else.
   National Suicide Hotline: 1-800-273-TALK (8255)
2. Sleeping less than 6 hours at night or feeling constantly fatigued.
3. Unable to care for daily needs or continuing to lose weight.
4. Isolating yourself from family and friends.
5. Overusing drugs, alcohol, food or money to numb the pain.
6. Feeling overwhelmed by other major life events.

About the Author: Rebecca S. Hauder, a Registered Nurse, Licensed Clinical Professional Counselor, and Marriage and Family Therapist in Boise, Idaho, worked numerous years in the hospice setting as a nurse and bereavement counselor. In her private practice, she has provided counseling to grieving persons since 1993. She leads frequent seminars on grief and has written a variety of bereavement resource materials for hospice organizations and funeral homes. Rebecca also serves as an adjunct professor for Boise State University's Department of Counselor Education and has a passion for photography, as seen on these pages.

The author, enjoying nature with her two grandchildren.

List of Photographs:

Made in the USA
Charleston, SC
10 November 2013